ALTERNATOR
BOOKS™

DESTINATION MARS

TRAVEL TO
MARS

Margaret J. Goldstein

Lerner Publications ◆ Minneapolis

Lerner Publications Company
An imprint of Lerner Publishing Group, Inc.
241 First Avenue North
Minneapolis, MN 55401 USA

For reading levels and more information, look up this title at www.lernerbooks.com.

Main body text set in Aptifer Sans LT Pro.
Typeface provided by Linotype AG.

Designer: Viet Chu **Photo Editor:** Cynthia Zemlicka

Library of Congress Cataloging-in-Publication Data

Names: Goldstein, Margaret J., author.
Title: Travel to Mars / Margaret J. Goldstein.
Description: Minneapolis : Lerner Publications, [2024] | Series: Destination Mars.
   Alternator books | Includes bibliographical references and index. | Audience:
   Ages 8–12 | Audience: Grades 4–6 | Summary: "Readers who've wondered how
   long it would take to get to Mars and how humans would survive such a trip will
   love delving into this book all about Mars travel!"— Provided by publisher.
Identifiers: LCCN 2022046109 (print) | LCCN 2022046110 (ebook) |
   ISBN 9781728490687 (library binding) | ISBN 9798765602805 (paperback) |
   ISBN 9781728496986 (ebook)
Subjects: LCSH: Space flight to Mars—Juvenile literature. | Manned space flight—
   Juvenile literature. | Mars (Planet)—Exploration—Juvenile literature.
Classification: LCC TL799.M3 G654 2024 (print) | LCC TL799.M3 (ebook) |
   DDC 629.45/53—dc23/eng/20230103

LC record available at https://lccn.loc.gov/2022046109
LC ebook record available at https://lccn.loc.gov/2022046110

Manufactured in the United States of America
1-52999-51017-2/24/2023

TABLE OF CONTENTS

Before astronauts use Orion to travel to Mars, NASA needs to make sure Orion works for missions to the moon. If successful, humans will return to the moon for the first time in many decades.

INTRODUCTION

DESTINATION MARS

Sometime in the 2030s or 2040s, a team of astronauts will take an unforgettable trip. It will start at the Kennedy Space Center in Cape Canaveral, Florida. There the astronauts will climb inside a spacecraft called Orion that sits on top of a powerful, 322-foot-tall (98 m) rocket.

Technicians will strap the astronauts tightly into their seats and wish them luck. When all preflight checks are complete, the rocket will blast through Earth's atmosphere, carrying Orion and the astronauts out into space. After three days of travel, Orion will dock at Gateway, a space station orbiting Earth's moon.

At Gateway the Orion astronauts will meet with scientists studying the moon. But they won't stay at the space station for long. Soon they will climb back inside Orion and embark on a muc longer journey. This trip will take them tens of millions of miles into the blackness of space. It will take them where no humans have ever gone before.

Orion will travel for at least six months to reach its destination. If the trip is successful and the astronauts arrive safely, they will be the first humans to visit Mars.

NASA tested its most powerful rocket ever, Artemis, on November 16, 2022. Artemis carried the Orion spacecraft through space for twenty-five days before returning to Earth.

Of all the planets in the solar system, scientists believe that Mars is the most like Earth.

Neptune

Uranus

Saturn

Jupiter

Mars

Earth

Venus

Mercury

CHAPTER 1

OUR NEIGHBOR IN SPACE

Mars is the fourth planet from the sun. Earth is third from the sun, so Mars is one of our nearest neighbors in space. It is a cold and rocky planet, with water ice at its north and south poles. It has a thin atmosphere made mostly of carbon dioxide. The Martian surface contains a lot of iron, which has a reddish color. This iron gives Mars its nickname: the Red Planet.

For thousands of years, humans have been curious about Mars. Ancient people saw it in the night sky. In the 1600s, people started looking at Mars with telescopes. They wanted to learn more about Mars.

Galileo Galilei (1564–1642) used telescopes to make many discoveries about Mars and other planets in our solar system.

In the mid-twentieth century, humans began to explore space. With astronauts at the helm, spacecraft orbited Earth and landed on the moon. Spacecraft controlled by people on Earth explored other parts of the solar system. Mariner 9, an

Mariner 9 took thousands of photographs of Mars's surface, giving scientists a look at the Red Planet they had never seen before.

Viking 2 was a lander, not a rover. It was stuck in one place once it landed. But it still collected a lot of important data.

orbiter, reached Mars in 1971. Viking 1 and 2 landed on Mars in 1976. Since then many more remote-control vehicles have visited Mars.

AT WORK ON MARS

Eight orbiters circle Mars in space. They create maps of Mars, analyze gases in its atmosphere, and measure its gravity. Rovers and other machines are on the surface of Mars. They take pictures, dig up soil samples, and study the Martian interior.

The Viking landers were sent to Mars's surface from orbiters. The orbiters took many images and measurements of Mars.

The Perseverance rover landed on Mars in 2021. It is looking for evidence of past life.

The vehicles on Mars have onboard computers, cameras, and scientific instruments. The vehicles send pictures and data to scientists on Earth using radio signals. By studying this information, scientists have pieced together the history of Mars. They believe that when Mars was young, more than four billion years ago, it was covered with rivers, lakes, and seas. It also had a thicker atmosphere. During this time, Mars might have been home to living things. The machines and scientists studying Mars are looking for signs of ancient life there.

Astronauts can help repair rovers and do many kinds of scientific experiments that machines cannot.

CHAPTER 2

ADDING ASTRONAUTS

To learn even more about Mars, space agencies want to send human visitors there. Humans can do tasks and gather information that machines cannot. Astronauts will be able to investigate Martian soil samples with their own eyes and hands. They will hear the Martian wind. They will smell gases in the Martian atmosphere. They will run experiments at laboratories on Mars itself or on orbiters circling the planet. Astronauts will drive rovers across Mars and explore the planet on foot. They will work with mission controllers to decide what to study and where to travel.

Seeing Mars up close will be a unique experience for any humans who get the chance to travel there.

THE MARTIAN FLEET

The United States National Aeronautics and Space Administration (NASA) is preparing the new spacecraft Orion for journeys to the moon and onward to Mars. In Orion's crew capsule, astronauts will look at computer monitors, communicate with mission controllers, operate instruments, and do other work to keep the spacecraft working properly as it travels. Out in space, larger living quarters will be attached to the crew capsule. This part of the craft will contain areas for sleeping, eating, exercising, and washing.

Matthias Maurer, an astronaut, stands next to a model of Orion's crew capsule. It can fit up to six astronauts.

SPACE OUTPOSTS

At space stations, astronauts live and study in space. Work on the International Space Station (ISS), which orbits Earth, includes studying the effects of weightlessness on the human body. On Gateway, which will orbit the moon, astronauts will study radiation and other kinds of energy. They will also travel from Gateway to the moon and back. When astronauts visit Mars, they will use a similar space station.

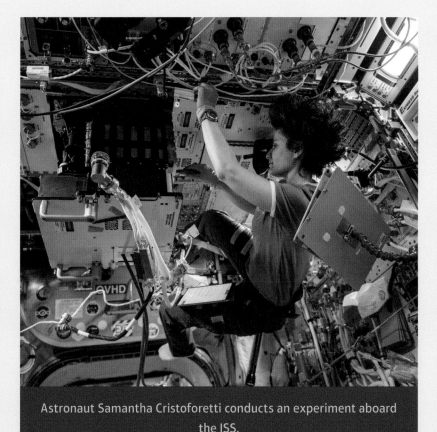

Astronaut Samantha Cristoforetti conducts an experiment aboard the ISS.

Orion is just one piece of the puzzle when it comes to putting astronauts on Mars. Unpiloted spacecraft will also be needed. For instance, when the astronauts reach Mars, they won't descend to its surface right away. They will first stop at an orbiting base camp. This large space station will hold laboratories, scientific instruments, and other technology.

MARS ORBITING BASE CAMP

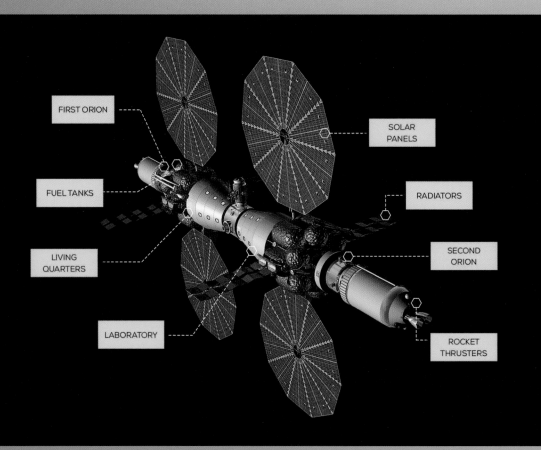

FIRST ORION

SOLAR PANELS

FUEL TANKS

RADIATORS

LIVING QUARTERS

SECOND ORION

LABORATORY

ROCKET THRUSTERS

In a 2021 NASA contest, college students used 3D printers to build models of their ideas for a space base. The contest helped NASA come up with new ideas for real space bases.

Descent vehicles docked at the station will carry astronauts to the Martian surface. NASA will send the base camp and other equipment to Mars before Orion and the astronauts arrive.

On the Martian surface, astronauts will need shelters to protect them from deadly radiation and extremely cold temperatures. They will need machines to make and store oxygen so they can breathe. Remote-control spacecraft will take supplies and building materials to Mars before Orion gets there. Robots might do the work of building shelters on the Martian surface. When astronauts arrive, their new homes will be ready.

In space, astronauts have to eat prepackaged food. But there are many different options available, such as pizza.

CHAPTER 3
AT HOME IN SPACE

Living in space is very different than living on Earth. In space there's no gravity to keep your feet on the floor or your rear end in a chair. Astronauts buckle themselves into seats, hold onto fixed objects, and use Velcro and other fasteners to keep themselves from floating around the inside of a spacecraft.

Astronauts live in zero gravity on the ISS, and engineers have created many tools to help them with their daily tasks. These same tools will help astronauts on Orion. For example, ordinary drinking cups don't work in space because in zero gravity, blobs of liquid float into the air instead of staying inside cups. Astronauts on Orion will drink from covered containers, sucking the liquid through straws or spouts. Astronauts will sleep inside sacks attached to the spacecraft walls. The sacks will keep sleeping astronauts from floating

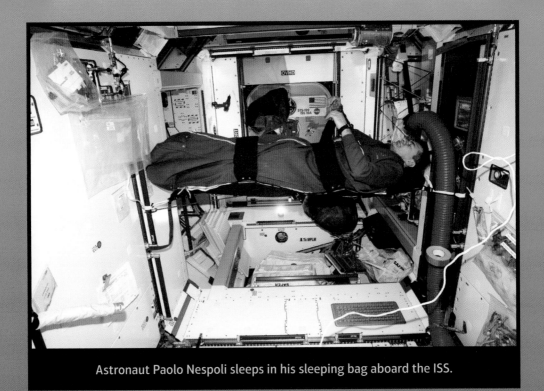

Astronaut Paolo Nespoli sleeps in his sleeping bag aboard the ISS.

away from their beds. Astronauts will use toilets that suction waste away from their bodies and into sealed containers.

LIFE SUPPORT

In space there's no air to breathe. Temperatures in space can be as low as −250°F (−157°C) and as high as 250°F (121°C). Orion and other spacecraft keep astronauts safe and healthy in the hostile world of space. On the trip to Mars, Orion's oxygen tanks will give astronauts the air they need to breathe. Heating and cooling systems will make sure the spacecraft isn't too cold or too hot.

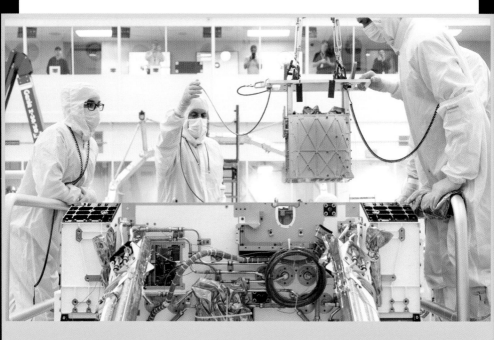

The golden box is MOXIE, a machine that converts Martian air into breathable air. NASA is testing MOXIE aboard the Perseverance rover. A larger version may one day help humans breathe on Mars.

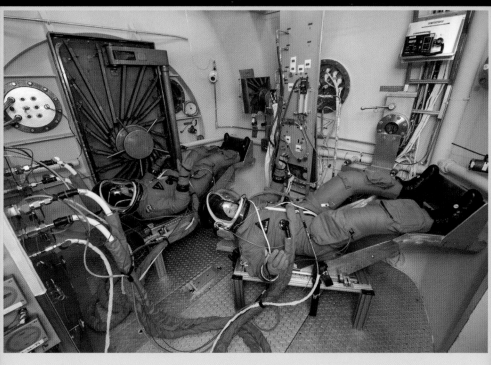
NASA designed new spacesuits for astronauts to wear aboard Orion.

In some ways, Orion will be different from near-Earth spacecraft like the ISS. When water, food, fuel, and oxygen supplies run low on the ISS, spacecraft can fly up from Earth and deliver more. This won't be possible for Orion, traveling millions of miles away from our planet. The craft will need to carry all the food, water, oxygen, medicine, and other materials astronauts need for their journey. To make supplies last, Orion will have recycling systems. One will turn leftover cooking and washing water into clean water for drinking. Another will convert carbon dioxide that astronauts exhale (breathe out) into oxygen they can inhale (breathe in).

Engineers work on a heat shield. The heat shield protects spacecraft as they descend through another planet's atmosphere.

CHAPTER 4

A DIFFICULT JOURNEY

A long space journey is risky and hazardous. Dangers include deadly radiation from the sun and other parts of space. To protect the astronauts inside, Orion will have strong radiation shielding.

The human body is designed to live on Earth, with gravity pulling us to the ground. On a spacecraft, with zero gravity the body undergoes changes. Muscles shrink and bones get thinner and weaker. Exercise helps counteract these changes. Orion will have treadmills, rowing machines, and other exercise equipment for astronauts.

Most astronauts return to Earth weighing a little less than when they left. NASA scientists are working on ways to help astronauts maintain a healthy weight in space.

BACK TO THE MOON

Between 1969 and 1972, astronauts landed on the moon six times. With NASA's Artemis project, astronauts will again visit the moon. They will descend from Gateway to study the moon's surface. Artemis will also serve as a testing ground for sending humans to Mars. Space agencies will test tools, spacesuits, shelters, and other technologies on the moon before sending astronauts to Mars.

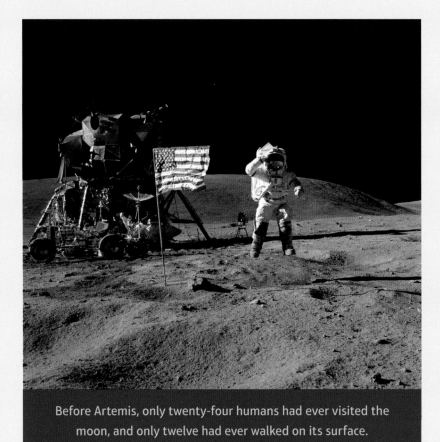

Before Artemis, only twenty-four humans had ever visited the moon, and only twelve had ever walked on its surface.

Astronauts aboard Orion will use new communication equipment to talk to scientists on Earth about the mission.

In the case of a medical emergency, astronauts could be in big trouble. They will have some medicines and medical devices on board. Some crew members will have medical training. But health care will be very limited on a spaceship, millions of miles from Earth and its hospitals.

HOMESICK

Like the other planets in our solar system, Mars and Earth orbit the sun. But they take different paths and travel at different speeds. The distance between them is always

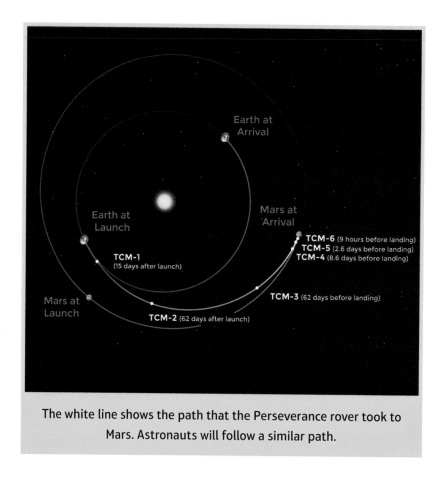

The white line shows the path that the Perseverance rover took to Mars. Astronauts will follow a similar path.

changing. For this reason, there's no set course between Earth and Mars. There's no set time frame for the trip either. It could take between six and nine months, depending on the speed of the spacecraft, the position of each planet during the journey, and the route chosen by mission planners.

After reaching Mars, astronauts will likely stay for several months before heading home. Space agencies say that altogether, Mars astronauts will be away from home for two to three years.

Mission planners worry about the toll on astronauts' mental health. Astronauts might feel frightened or lonely during the long journey. They will have other crew members to talk to, but they will likely miss their friends and family. It won't be easy to phone home because the farther a spacecraft gets

Mission planners meet with astronauts often to check on their health.

from Earth, the longer it takes for radio signals to travel back and forth. An astronaut might speak to a loved one by phone and wait up to forty minutes for a response. Conversations will be difficult.

Space agencies are devising systems to help astronauts handle loneliness on the long Mars journey. Ideas include social robots to talk to astronauts and virtual reality devices to immerse them in the sights and sounds of home.

NASA is working on a new kind of communication system using lasers. Lasers can send larger amounts of information at once than radio signals can.

We may not know who the first person to visit Mars will be until many years from now.

Even with the best technology, visiting Mars will be risky, scary, and lonely. But for the first humans to set foot on Mars, it will be the trip of a lifetime.

Glossary

atmosphere: a layer of gases surrounding a planet

data: facts, statistics, and other information that can be studied

descent vehicle: a spacecraft that travels down to the surface of a planet or moon

dock: to join with another spacecraft in space

gravity: a force that pulls objects toward a planet, moon, or other object in space

orbit: to circle around something

radiation: energy that travels through space, some of which is deadly to living things

rover: a vehicle that drives over rough terrain

solar system: the sun and everything that circles it in space, including planets, asteroids, and moons

virtual reality: an environment that seems real but that is actually created by a computer

weightlessness: being in an environment without gravity

Learn More

ESA Kids
https://www.esa.int/kids/en/home

Hamilton, John. *Humans to Mars*. Minneapolis: Abdo & Daughters, 2019.

Kenny, Karen Latchana. *Cutting-Edge Astronaut Training*. Minneapolis: Lerner Publications, 2020.

NASA: Mars Exploration
https://mars.nasa.gov/participate/funzone/

NASA Space Place: Mars
https://spaceplace.nasa.gov/search/MARS/

NASA: What Is Orion?
https://www.nasa.gov/audience/forstudents/5-8/features/nasa
-knows/what-is-orion-58.html

Olson, Elsie. *Breakthroughs in Moon Exploration*. Minneapolis: Lerner Publications, 2020.

Olson, Elsie. *Spectacular Space Stations*. Minneapolis: Lerner Publications, 2020.

Index

Photo Acknowledgments

Image credits: NASA, pp. 4, 5, 8, 9, 10, 12, 15, 17, 18, 19, 20, 21, 22, 23, 24, 25, 27, 28;
Steve Allen/Getty Images, p. 6; Photos.com/Getty Images, p. 7; NASA/JPL-Caltech,
pp. 11, 26; dottedhippo/Getty Images, p. 13; Felix Hörhager/picture alliance/Getty
Images, p. 14; Lockheed Martin Corporation, p. 16; 3DSculptor/Getty Images, p. 29.
Design elements: Tiradae Manyum/EyeEm/Getty Images; ESA/DLR/FU-Berlin.

Front cover: 3DSculptor/Getty Images.